Tillie Makes a Friend

Book 1 of the *Pup Tales* Series

By Nancy Nelson
Illustrated by Becky Wosick

atmosphere press

There once was a dog called Tillie.
Her name was really quite silly.
With curly white fur and eyes that shone blue,
She should have been named something like Sue.

Her long floppy ears swung down to the ground;
She weighed in at twenty and one half a pound.
Her legs they were short, her tail even smaller.
If only she'd grown just five inches taller.

With a little more height she might have been able
To snag all the food from the plates on the table.
A little more height would give her an edge
Over the nasty big dog, beyond the back hedge.

His bark it was big, his growl deep and low.
She'd heard someone call him "Big Bad Bo."
Bo sounded scary and always so mad.
Tillie was frightened but also felt sad.

Why was Bo barking most days and some nights?
Didn't he know it just wasn't right?
Tillie had learned, thanks to her master,
There were much better ways of getting things faster.

If she needed to get out or go for a walk,
She used her own version of sweet doggie talk.
Two little barks and one long, low whine,
And she got what she wanted every time.

When she sat on command and offered her paw,
She'd get a big bone on which she could gnaw.
Tillie liked her dog life, and just didn't know
What was it like for the barking dog Bo.

What was so wrong?
Why the loud bark?
Maybe he needed a walk in the park.
Was his collar too tight
or his yard just too small?
Did he need some new toys?
A bone or a ball?

Perhaps he was sick of being alone,
Or maybe he wanted a new doggie home.
His owners were Mikey and Millie McQuirk.
Tillie would see them leaving for work.

From what she had seen from behind the dog gate,
They always looked to be running a little bit late.
Her hair was a mess, his tie was askew.
They'd jump in their cars and bid Bo adieu.

What could she do?
How could she help?
Maybe a sweet "I get it" yelp?
She trotted on over
to the edge of the yard,
Cautious and careful, keeping her guard.

What would Bo look like,
and would he be nice?
Close to her size,
or bigger than twice?
She inched ever closer
and here's what she saw:
Black beady eyes
and a big toothy jaw.

Bo let out a snarl and Tillie jumped back,
Nervous the beast soon would attack.
The bushes then rustled; the branches were parted.
Was a bad doggie fight about to be started?

Wide-eyed with fear, now frozen in place,
All she could see was Bo's big doggie face.
Bo gave her a smile and with a tilt of his head,
Let Tillie know she had nothing to dread.

They stared at each other a minute or two,
And suddenly Tillie knew just what to do.
She picked up a bone that she'd left in the grass,
And to her new friend she quickly did pass.

Bo took the bone and started to chew,
And Tillie was happy because she now knew.
Bo wasn't scary, too mean, or too tall.
He just needed a friend; that was all.

About the Author

Born and bred in the Chicago suburbs, Nancy was raised with two cats, a half dozen turtles and Sneakers the Schnoodle.

She went to college in Cleveland, enjoyed a career as a newspaper reporter, columnist and editor, raised five children and an assortment of precocious pooches.

These are some of their stories.

About the Illustrator

From a young age Becky loved to draw, paint, and think creatively. Bringing stories to life through illustration has been a passion of hers for a long time.

Becky lives in Wisconsin with her husband, three young kids, and a goofy pup who helps inspire her dog drawings!

When Becky isn't creating, she enjoys adventures with her family, working on home improvement projects, and being outdoors

About Atmosphere Press

Atmosphere Press is an independent, full-service publisher for excellent books in all genres and for all audiences. Learn more about what we do at atmospherepress.com.

We encourage you to check out some of Atmosphere's latest releases, which are available at Amazon.com and via order from your local bookstore:

Yellow Yuba, by Jocelyn Tambascio
Alley: I Have Albinism, by Alethea Allen
Santa on a Surfboard, by Laura Sharp
Lilah Loves Life, by Brian Sullivan
The Christmas Witch, by Jaime Katusha
My Sister is Sick . . . What About Me?, by Mary Kay and Eli Olson
There's a Spider in My Bed, by Devon Nunnally and Biaina Alexanian
Yikes, I Saw a Barracuda!, by Tamara Anderson
Winston's Big Wind, by Barbara Reyelts
Twinkle Toes, by Connie Jameson
The Tail of a Trio, by Katherine Scott
Cow Days, by Christina Warfel
Logan and Lexi Meditate, by Denesia D. Rogers

www.ingramcontent.com/pod-product-compliance
Lightning Source LLC
LaVergne TN
LVHW070447070526
838199LV00037B/718